Becoming VESSELS OF HIS MERCIES

DESMOND MAMBU YARJAH

ISBN:
978-9970-925-00-1

Author's Information

email: dmyarjah20@gmail.com
Instagram: dyarjah
FB: Desmond Enoch Mambu Yarjah
Phone number: +233 (0) 245698367

Designed & Printed by
Supreme Brandoor
+233 (0) 241 163 474
supremebrandoor@yahoo.com

DEDICATION

This book is dedicated to the Holy Spirit, the fountain of all wisdom.

FOREWORD

In a world often filled with judgment, division, and pain, there is a profound longing for mercy. We yearn for a sanctuary where forgiveness, compassion, and grace reign supreme. In "Becoming Vessels of His Mercy," Desmond Yarjah offers us a guiding light, illuminating the path to becoming vessels through which God's mercy flows.

With wisdom born from personal experiences and a deep understanding of God's character, Desmond invites us on a transformative journey. Through the pages of this remarkable book, he reveals the power of mercy to heal wounds, reconcile relationships, and restore hope.

Desmond reminds us that we are not defined by our mistakes or shortcomings, but rather by the boundless love and mercy of our Creator. He paints a vivid picture of a world where mercy transcends barriers, where no one is left behind, and where the transformative power of grace reaches the deepest recesses of our souls.

In *"Becoming Vessels of His Mercy,"* Desmond's words resonate with authenticity, compassion, and a profound faith in the transformative nature of divine mercy. He guides us through the depths of what it means to be vessels, vessels that carry and pour out the life-giving stream of mercy onto a world desperately in need of it.

As you embark on this journey with Desmond, open your heart and soul to the profound truth that you too can become a vessel of His mercy. Let the words on these pages ignite a spark within you, compelling you to embrace and share the immeasurable grace that flows abundantly from the heart of God.

Prepare to be inspired, uplifted, and forever changed as you step into the powerful and sacred calling of becoming vessels of His mercy. May this book be a guiding light, leading you to a life filled with love, forgiveness, and the remarkable transformation that comes from embracing and extending divine mercy.

Let the journey begin.

Elizabeth Samuel,
Book Project Consultant.

TABLE OF CONTENTS

INTRODUCTION
DIVINE MERCY IS AN ASSET

"God's mercy is bigger than any mistake. He not only turns bad situations around, he causes something good to come out if it." - Joel Osteen

The mercy of God is a powerful asset in the journey of life. It determines our impact and existence on earth. We are alive because of His mercy. Every morning we wake up is a result of God's merciful provision. We are not alive because we deserve it, but because

His mercy is at work.

Lamentations 3:22-23 says, ***"It is by the Lord's mercies that we are not consumed, because His compassions fail not. They are new every morning; great is His faithfulness."***

Many of us, who are alive today, have given Satan too many opportunities to consume us, but God's mercy has prevented it.

God's mercy is so powerful that it can override judgment. It can transform a mess into a message and a sinner into a saint. Despite our frequent rebellion and disobedience to His commandments, we have not received the punishment we deserve. It is not because of our intelligence or smartness, but because God chooses to forgive our sins through His love and mercy.

If God was to punish us according to our sins, it is doubtful anyone would be alive today. Psalm 130:3-4 says, ***"If You, Lord, should mark iniquities, O Lord, who could stand? But there is forgiveness with You, that You may be feared."*** When God forgives, He does not keep a record of our sins.

Psalm 103:1-12, ***with special attention to verses 10-12 says, "He has not dealt with us according to our sins, nor punished us according to our iniquities. For as the heavens are high above the earth, so great is His mercy toward those who fear Him; as far as the east is from the west, so far has He removed our transgressions from us."***

You need to understand that God is a merciful friend. However, let me clarify that

God does not tolerate sin. His mercy is provided to help us turn away from our sins. God does not want us to continue in sin; that's why His mercy is available to erase the record of sin.

Do you think your sin is too great to be forgiven? No matter how grave your sins may be, God's mercies are even greater. You do not need to persist in that sin, my friend. Reach out for His mercy today, and you will be forgiven.

God's forgiveness is not based on the magnitude of your sins, but on His loving kindness and tenderness. Just like Saul of Tarsus, who orchestrated the persecution of Christians and authorized the stoning of Stephen, obtained mercy from God and became one of the greatest Apostles to have ever lived on earth.

Through the mercies of God, Paul's destiny was repositioned, and his life was completely transformed for God's eternal glory. Like Saul, there is hope for you. Your life is meant to change for the better. God is ready to realign your destiny for greatness.

All you need to do is confess your sins before God, turn away from them, and you will experience the abundant mercies of God. Join me as we explore the depths of God's mercies.

CHAPTER ONE
WHAT IS MERCY?

"Mercy is the stuff you give to people that don't deserve it." - Joyce Meyer

The mercy of God is not a license to continue sinning, but rather God's redemptive plan to escape impending judgment for wrongdoing. According to Webster's Dictionary, mercy is defined as *"the ability to refrain from harming or punishing offenders, enemies, or persons in one's power."*

1) The mercy of God is the forgiveness extended to those who deserve punishment for their wrong actions.

It is when you have knowingly done something wrong and you are to face the consequences, but instead of receiving judgment, mercy intervenes on your behalf. Where mercy exists, judgment cannot prevail. The arrival of God's mercy disappoints judgment, and mercy always triumphs over judgment.

Matthew 9:13 states, ***"But go ye and learn what that meaneth, I will have mercy, and not sacrifice: for I am not come to call the righteous, but sinners to repentance."*** When God's mercy is at work, judgment holds no power. In the presence of mercy, forgiveness is guaranteed.

2) Mercy is an extension of God's love and kindness toward humanity.

3) Mercy is God's gift of a repentant heart.

Psalm 86:5 says, ***"For thou, Lord, art good, and ready to forgive, and plenteous in mercy unto all them that call upon thee."*** When we confess our sins and turn away from them, God extends His mercy to us. God is ready to forgive any sin, but genuine repentance is required. When God sees a repentant heart, He pours out His mercies.

Many people today confess their sins but resist true repentance, thereby hindering the entrance of God's mercy into their lives. If you desire to experience His mercies, be prepared to repent. Genuine repentance attracts God's mercy, regardless of the severity of the wrong committed.

4) Mercy is the act of withholding deserved judgment for wrongdoing.

The story in John 8:1-11 illustrates this concept. Jesus went to the Mount of Olives, and early in the morning, He entered the temple where people gathered around Him to listen to His teachings. The scribes and Pharisees brought a woman caught in adultery and presented her to Jesus, stating that according to the law of Moses, she should be stoned.

They posed this question to test Jesus and find an accusation against Him. However, Jesus stooped down and began writing on the ground, seemingly ignoring their words. When they persistently questioned Him, He stood up and said, ***"Let he who is without sin*** *among you be the first to throw a stone at her."*

Then He stooped down and continued writing on the ground. One by one, starting with the eldest, those who heard His words and were convicted by their own conscience left. Eventually, only Jesus and the woman remained. Jesus asked her, *"Where are your accusers? Has no one condemned you?"* She replied, *"No one, Lord."* And Jesus said, *"Neither do I condemn you. Go and sin no more."*

5) Mercy is the outpouring of God's compassion that closes the door to His judgment. When God manifests His mercy, the door to judgment is shut.

6) Mercy is an expression of God's goodwill toward humanity.

7) Mercy is God's plan for mankind's redemption from sin. God showed us mercy when He sacrificially sent Jesus for our sake.

8) Mercy is a compassionate response from someone who possesses the power to punish or judge.

WHY WE NEED THE MERCY OF GOD

I) Salvation is impossible without the mercy of God:

In Ephesians 2:4-5, it is stated, ***"But God, who is rich in mercy, because of His great love with which He loved us, even when we were dead in trespasses, made us alive together with Christ (by grace you have been saved)."*** The mercies of God played a crucial role in the sacrifice of Jesus Christ on the cross.

Without God's mercies, the purpose of Calvary would have been impossible. Salvation is intricately connected to God's mercies. Through the mercies achieved on the cross, sinners who genuinely confess their sins and repent are instantly forgiven. We are saved by His mercies.

II) God does not desire hell for His people:

In 2 Peter 3:9, it is expressed, ***"The Lord is not slack concerning His promise, as some count slackness, but is longsuffering toward us, not willing that any should perish but that all should come to repentance."*** Hell was never intended for humanity but for Satan and his followers.

Despite the great wickedness of Nineveh, God spared the city through His mercies. Jonah preached in Nineveh, proclaiming God's impending judgment. However, when the people repented, God responded with His mercies instead of judgment. Jonah was disappointed by God's forgiveness instead of judgment.

In today's world, there are preachers like Jonah who emphasize God's judgment rather than His forgiveness and the opportunity for people to draw closer to Him. God did not call us to proclaim judgment upon His people; He called us to lead His people to the cross. His desire is for them to be saved, not to perish in their sins.

Friend, God does not delight in the destruction of humanity. He is interested in your salvation, not your death. You do not have to perish in your sins. Come to Jesus, draw nearer to the cross, and His mercy will deliver you from sin. God is merciful. Regardless of the sin committed, forgiveness is still possible if one is willing to repent. The devil's strength lies in man's unwillingness to repent.

In Ezekiel 18:23 and 32, it is said, ***"Do I***

have any pleasure at all that the wicked should die?" says the Lord God, "and not that he should turn from his ways and live?" "For I have no pleasure in the death of one who dies," says the Lord God. "Therefore turn and live!"

The repentance of Nineveh pleased God. In Jonah 4:1-4, Jonah was displeased and angry about God's mercy towards Nineveh. He prayed to the Lord, expressing his dissatisfaction. However, God questioned Jonah's anger. God bestows His mercies upon those who turn from their wickedness.

To the person reading this book, you deserve mercies and not judgment. Reach out now for His mercies. Bow your head and say this prayer, *"Lord Jesus, I confess that I am a sinner. Please forgive me, wash me with Your precious blood, and come into my life. I repent of my sins. Save me, as I cannot save myself, and establish me in the faith."*

Congratulations! In the name of Jesus, you will not be destroyed. I see God rebranding your life, just like Paul's transformation.

III) Without the mercies of God, Satan would have consumed many of us:

The mercies of God have been our refuge, protecting us from the devouring schemes of Satan. In Lamentations 3:22, it is written, ***"Through the Lord's mercies we are not consumed because His compassions fail not."*** Satan, being merciless, takes pleasure in the destruction of humanity.

As said in John 10:10, ***"The thief does not come except to steal, and to kill, and to destroy."*** However, God, in His great love, sent His Son to offer us life in abundance. The mercies of God act as a shield against the perils of the devil. Without God's mercies, many of us would have fallen prey to the enemy's schemes.

In Psalm 143:2, it is said, ***"Do not enter into judgment with Your servant, for in Your sight no one living is righteous."*** We owe our gratitude to the mercies of God for sparing us from the wickedness of the devil. Truly, God's mercy knows no bounds. He has graciously overlooked our multitude of errors and shortcomings.

If not for His mercy, individuals like Paul and David would not have experienced redemption and restoration. Their lives stand as a testament to the transformative power of God's mercy.

CHAPTER TWO
THE DIVINE ASPECTS OF GOD'S MERCY

"God's mercy and grace give me hope, for myself, and for our world." - Billy Graham

1) GOD IS MERCIFUL:

To be merciful means to be full of mercy. The mercies of God are inexhaustible and infinite. 2 Corinthians 1:3 says, ***"Blessed be God, even the father of our Lord Jesus***

Christ, the Father of mercies, and the God of all comfort." If God was not full of mercies, many of us would have received instant judgement.

How many times have we erred and still returned to God, saying, *"Father, have mercy?"* He does not keep count of the many mercies you have taken from His throne. He is always ready to release another mercy when you ask for it.

2) GOD'S MERCIES ARE NEVER-ENDING:

They have no end as long as you are breathing. So, take advantage of His mercies to save yourself from sin. Psalms 103:17 says, ***"But the mercy of the LORD is from everlasting to everlasting upon them that fear him, and his righteousness unto*** *children's children."*

3) GOD'S MERCY ENDURES

In Psalms 136:1-26, it is written, ***"O give thanks unto the LORD; for he is good: for his mercy endureth for ever."*** This passage continues to emphasize the enduring nature of God's mercy. When God forgives you, He does not withdraw that forgiveness.

When you sin and ask God for His mercy He forgives you. Do not allow Satan to hold you captive by your past sins when you have repented. If the devil brings guilt after repentance, remind him that God's mercies endure forever. His mercy will always prevail.

4) GOD'S MERCY IS GREAT:

God' mercy surpasses any kind of sin. Your sin may be great, but God's mercy is greater and can wipe out your sins. The greatness of God's mercy can overcome the greatest sin you have ever committed. Even if you have gone deep into sin, the greatness of God's mercy can pull you out of that ocean of sin.

Some people believe they will never be forgiven because of the depth and magnitude of their sins. Do not believe that lie; you can be forgiven right now through the greatness of God's mercies. I see God's mercies prevailing over every sin in your life right now.

In Psalms 145:8, it is written, *"The LORD is gracious, and full of compassion; slow to anger, and of great mercy."* Additionally, in 2 Samuel 24:14, David says to God, *"I am in great strait: let us fall now into the hand of the LORD; for his mercies are great: and let me not fall into the hand of men."*

5) GOD'S MERCY IS ABUNDANT:

Psalms 103:8 says, ***"The LORD is merciful and gracious, slow to anger, and plenteous in mercy."*** The mercies of God are available in great quantity and are inexhaustible. You can receive as much mercy as you need. Mercy is an inexhaustible virtue.

6) GOD'S MERCY IS NEW EVERY MORNING:

Lamentations 3:22 says, ***"It is of the LORD'S mercy that we are not consumed because his compassions fail not."*** God's mercy is renewed daily. Each new day signifies the release of fresh mercies in your life. So, every time you see another day, it is an indication of new mercies released in your direction.

7) GOD SUPPLIES HIS MERCY TO ALL:

God extends His mercies to all who call upon Him. He hears the prayers and supplications of His servants. References such as Psalms 6:9, 1 Kings 8:28, 2 Chronicles 6:19, and Job 9:15 highlight the importance of prayer and supplication in receiving God's mercy.

8) GOD IS COMPASSIONATE:

Psalms 86:15 says, ***"But thou, O Lord, art a God full of compassion, and gracious,*** *longsuffering, and plenteous in mercy and truth. "* Matthew 9:36 also emphasizes Jesus' compassion for the multitudes. His compassion extends to those who are weary and lost.

9) GOD IS SLOW TO ANGER:

Nehemiah 1:3, Psalms 103:8-10, Nehemiah 9:7, and Joel 2:13 all highlight God's patience and long-suffering nature. He gives humanity the opportunity to turn away from their wickedness and repent. His anger is restrained for the purpose of repentance.

10) GOD IS RICH IN MERCY

Ephesians 2:4-5 says, *"But God, who is rich in mercy, for his great love wherewith he loved us, even when we were dead in sins, hath quickened us together with Christ."* God's richness in mercy allows Him to pour out His mercies in abundant measures. His love and mercy are not limited.

11) GOD'S MERCY IS ETERNAL:

The mercy of God is eternal and unchanging. Psalms 66:20 declares, *"Blessed be God, which hath not turned away my prayer, nor his mercy from me."* God's mercy is everlasting and remains steadfast.

CHAPTER THREE

INSPIRING SCRIPTURAL ENCOUNTERS WITH GOD'S MERCIFUL NATURE

"Your sin is not greater than God's mercy. God's mercy is fresh and new every morning." - Norman Khan

1) Abraham's Deception and God's Mercy

In Genesis 20:1-5, we witnessed Abraham's journey to the southern region, where he settled between Kadesh and Shur, residing in Gerar. Unfortunately, Abraham resorts to deception by claiming Sarah, his wife, is his sister.

Consequently, Abimelech, the king of Gerar, unknowingly takes Sarah into his household. However, God intervenes, warning Abimelech through a dream, revealing that Sarah is indeed married. Abimelech, who had not approached her intimately, pleads for mercy, expressing concern for his righteous nation.

He justifies his actions by recounting that Abraham and Sarah both referred to each other as siblings. Despite this misrepresentation, Abimelech claims innocence. Here, the mercy of God prevails, sparing Abraham from severe consequences.

2) The Woman Caught in Adultery

John 8:10-11 recounts an incident involving Jesus and a woman caught in the act of adultery. The Jewish law mandated stoning as punishment for such offenses. However, Jesus, driven by compassion and mercy, challenges her accusers, asking if any among them condemn her.

As they depart one by one, Jesus addresses the woman, who affirms that no one condemns her. Jesus, without condemnation Himself, instructs her to sin no more. Through His mercy, the woman experiences not death but a chance for a new life.

3) Saul's Transformation into Apostle Paul

In 1 Timothy 1:16, Paul reflects on his past as Saul, a persecutor of Christians. He acknowledges that it was by the mercy of God that he obtained salvation, serving as a demonstration of Jesus Christ's immense patience and long suffering.

Acts 8:1 and 9:1-6 illustrate Saul's brutal actions, including consenting to the execution of believers, instigating persecution, and seeking authority to capture followers of Jesus. However, during his journey to Damascus, a heavenly light appears, and Jesus confronts Saul, questioning his persecution. Trembling and astonished, Saul recognizes Jesus as Lord and asks what he should do.

Jesus commands him to go into the city and await further instructions. This transformative encounter leads to Saul's conversion and eventual emergence as the esteemed Apostle Paul, a testament to the power of God's mercy.

4) The Thief on the Cross

Luke 23:37-43 recounts the crucifixion scene, with Jesus positioned between two criminals. One of the thieves mocks Jesus, challenging Him to save Himself and them. However, the other thief rebukes him, acknowledging their just condemnation and recognizing Jesus's innocence.

In his final moments, the repentant thief implores Jesus, *"Lord, remember me when you come into your kingdom."* Jesus, in His mercy, assures him that they will be together in paradise that very day. Despite deserving death and eternal damnation, the thief receives mercy at the eleventh hour, altering his eternal destiny.

Luke 23:42-43 says, *"And he said unto Jesus, Lord, remember me when thou comest into thy kingdom. And Jesus said unto him, Verily I say unto thee, Today shalt thou be with me in paradise."*

He was on his way to hell. He deserved death and hell, but at the point of death, he received mercy and that changed his eternal destination. Do not wait till you die, reach out for His mercy now, tomorrow might be too late.

5) David's Fall and God's Mercy

David, despite committing adultery and murder, received the mercy of God while becoming one of the greatest kings in Israel's history. This chapter explores David's transgressions, his plea for mercy, and the profound impact of God's forgiveness.

In 2 Samuel 1:1-4, we find David returning from battle after defeating the Amalekites. Shortly thereafter, a man arrives, bearing the tragic news of Saul and Jonathan's deaths. David's response to this news is captured in verses 26-27, where he mourns the loss of his beloved friend Jonathan and reflects on the fallen state of the mighty.

It is in these moments of distress that David recognizes the weight of his own sins. In Psalms 51:1-11, a psalm penned by David following a confrontation with the prophet Nathan regarding his adulterous affair with Bathsheba, we witness the depths of David's remorse and his earnest plea for mercy.

David acknowledges his transgressions and implores God to forgive him, acknowledging that his sins are ever before him. He recognizes that his actions were ultimately against God Himself and expresses his desire for cleansing, renewal, and restoration.

Throughout this psalm, David's heartfelt prayer demonstrates his deep understanding of God's character and his unwavering faith in His mercy. He longs for purification, seeking to be washed thoroughly from his iniquity and to have a clean heart and a right spirit restored within him. David humbly requests that God not cast him away and that His holy spirit remains with him.

The story of David's fall and subsequent plea for mercy showcases the profound transformative power of God's forgiveness.

Despite the gravity of his sins, David's repentance and genuine desire for reconciliation with God lead to a restoration of their relationship. God, in His abundant mercy, forgives David, enabling him to rise above his transgressions and fulfill his purpose as a king.

David's journey serves as a reminder that no matter how grave our sins may be, God's mercy is available to all who genuinely repent and seek His forgiveness. David's story teaches us that God's grace knows no bounds and that through sincere repentance, we too can experience the transformative power of His mercy.

As we reflect on David's life, let us learn from his example and embrace the mercy of God in our own lives. Just as David found redemption and continued to serve as a remarkable king, we too can find forgiveness and live a life dedicated to fulfilling God's purpose for us.

6) The Return of the Prodigal Son

In Luke 15:11-24, we encounter the parable of the prodigal son. The younger son demands his inheritance and recklessly squanders it in a far-off land. Reduced to poverty and despair, he realizes the error of his ways and decides to return to his father's house. Filled with remorse, he plans to confess his sins and ask to be treated as a hired servant rather than a son.

Yet, upon his arrival, his father, filled with compassion, runs to embrace him, orders a celebration, and reinstates him as his beloved son. This story illustrates the boundless mercy and love of the father, who eagerly forgives and restores his wayward child.

The prodigal son's journey portrays the loving and forgiving nature of God, who eagerly receives and restores those who return to Him with contrite hearts. This account encourages us not to lose hope, regardless of our past mistakes or the depth of our sins. God's mercy knows no bounds, and through genuine repentance, we can experience His transformative forgiveness.

Let us learn from the prodigal son and embrace the mercy of God in our own lives. May we humbly seek His forgiveness, knowing that His compassion and grace can change our lives and restore us to a right relationship with Him.

7) The surprising mercy extended to the wicked King Ahab.

In 1 Kings 21:17-29, we encountered the wicked King Ahab, who committed heinous acts, including murder and the theft of Naboth's vineyard. God sends the prophet Elijah to confront Ahab, pronouncing severe judgment upon him and his household.

However, when Ahab humbled himself before the Lord, wearing sackcloth and fasting, God recognized his genuine repentance. In response, God shows mercy to Ahab, deferring the pronounced judgment to the days of his descendants. This account highlights God's willingness to extend mercy to those who genuinely repent, even in the face of their grievous sins.

This story illustrates the profound impact of genuine repentance and the willingness of God to extend mercy to those who seek it. Ahab's story serves as a reminder that even the most wicked individuals can find mercy if they sincerely humble themselves before God.

8) Peter received mercy

Peter, known for his impulsive nature, famously denied Jesus three times in Matthew 26:69-75. Yet, after Jesus' resurrection, Peter received mercy and forgiveness. God used him mightily to proclaim the Gospel, and through his preaching, thousands of souls were won for Christ. Peter's story reminds us that no matter how grievous our mistakes, God's mercy is available to transform and redeem us.

9) Moses received mercy

Moses, in Exodus 3:11, displayed moments of stubbornness and doubt when confronted with God's call to lead the Israelites out of Egypt. Despite his initial hesitations, God showed mercy to Moses and used him to deliver His people from bondage.

Through God's guidance, Moses became one of the greatest leaders in biblical history, displaying courage and faithfulness. His story teaches us that God's mercy can overcome our insecurities and equip us for His purposes.

9) Rahab received mercy

Rahab, once a prostitute, found mercy and

grace from God in Joshua 2:1-21. Through her act of faith and protection of the Israelite spies, she and her family were spared during the conquest of Jericho. Rahab's life was radically transformed, and she became part of the lineage of Jesus Christ, serving as a testament to God's redemptive mercy.

10) Jacob received mercy

Jacob, known for his deceitful nature, encountered God's mercy and underwent a transformation. Through wrestling with God in Genesis 32:22-32, Jacob received both physical and spiritual healing, and his name was changed to Israel. Despite his past actions, God's mercy prevailed, and Jacob became an integral figure in the history of God's people.

11) The blind Bartimaeus received mercy

Blind Bartimaeus, as depicted in Mark 10:46-52, illustrates the compassionate mercy of Jesus. Despite his physical blindness and societal marginalization, Bartimaeus cried out to Jesus for mercy, recognizing Him as the Son of David.

Jesus, moved by Bartimaeus' faith, healed his blindness and granted him a new life. Bartimaeus's story highlights that no matter our circumstances, God's merciful touch can bring transformation and restoration.

12) Joseph received mercy

Joseph, in Genesis 39:21, experienced God's mercy throughout his challenging journey. Instead of being killed by his brothers, he was sold into slavery, eventually rising to a position of authority in Potiphar's house.

Even when he was unjustly imprisoned, God's mercy remained with him, as evidenced by the favor he found in the eyes of the prison keeper. Joseph's story teaches us that God's mercy can guide us through difficult circumstances and ultimately lead us to fulfill our divine destiny.

13) The Lunatic Boy received mercy

In Matthew 17:14-18, the father of a boy possessed by a spirit sought mercy from Jesus. Despite the disciples' initial inability to heal the boy, Jesus demonstrated compassion and mercy by delivering him from the demonic oppression. This account serves as a reminder that God's mercy is available to those who earnestly seek Him and intercede on behalf of others.

The unchanging nature of God's mercy is emphasized in Malachi 3:6. Just as God showed His love and compassion to men and women in the past, He continues to extend His mercy to us today. His steadfast nature ensures that His mercies are not limited to specific times or individuals but are available to all who call upon Him.

14) Jonah received mercy

Jonah, in the midst of his disobedience, experienced the mercy of God. Even when swallowed by a great fish, God's mercy preserved his life and provided an opportunity for repentance and redemption. Jonah's story demonstrates that even in our darkest moments, God's mercy can lead us to restoration and renewed purpose.

15) The Israelites received mercy

The Israelites, despite their murmuring and complaints in the wilderness, witnessed God's merciful provision. In Exodus 16:3 and 16:12, God heard their cries and supplied them with food and water, reminding them of His faithfulness. This narrative serves as a reminder that God's mercy extends even to those who doubt and complain, displaying His patience and willingness to meet their needs.

These examples illustrate God's merciful nature and His desire to intervene in the lives of His people. The stories exemplify the transformative power of God's mercy

Whether through divine protection, healing, provision, or forgiveness, God's mercy remains constant and available to all who seek Him.

Just as all these people experienced God's mercies, we too can rely on His unwavering compassion. Let us embrace God's mercy, seek His forgiveness, and allow His transformative power to work in our lives. Let us approach Him with humble hearts, knowing that His mercies are never-ending and that He can turn our circumstances around for His glory.

CHAPTER FOUR

THE POWER OF GOD'S MERCY

"We must trust in the mighty power of God's mercy. We are all sinners, but His grace transforms us and makes us new." - Picture Quotes

1) The mercies of God preserve us from the schemes of the devil.

Lamentations 3:22-23 says, ***"It is of the Lord's mercies that we are not consumed*** *because his compassions fail not. They are new every morning: great is thy faithfulness."* When we encounter the mercy of God, we are protected from the destruction caused by the devil.

From this day forward, receive the mercies of God, which ensure that the enemy cannot prematurely end your life. By God's mercy, you will fulfill the number of your days on earth, escaping the wickedness of the enemy.

2) The mercy of God delivers us from affliction.

Mark 10:47-48 recounts the story of Bartimaeus, who cried out to Jesus, *"Jesus, thou Son of David, have mercy on me."* Despite others telling him to be quiet, he persisted in seeking God's mercy. Through the mercies of God, our pain is transformed into gain. God's mercy rescues us from the afflictions caused by the enemy.

3) The mercy of God brings healing and deliverance.

Matthew 17:14-18 tells the account of a father who brought his demon-possessed son to Jesus for healing. The disciples had been unable to cure the boy, but Jesus rebuked the devil, and the child was instantly healed.

Mercy is a powerful force that operates against sickness and disease. When God's mercy is released, sickness and disease cannot survive. The mercies of God can overcome any form of illness. Leprosy was cured by His mercies.

The mercies of God was also manifested in

the following passages:

Mark 1:40-42, where Jesus heals a leper with compassion and a touch.

Psalm 103:3, which emphasizes that God forgives our sins and heals our diseases.

James 5:14-15, which encourages us to call for the elders of the church to pray and anoint the sick with oil, believing in God's healing power.

Embrace the power of God's mercy in your life and experience deliverance, healing, and protection from the schemes of the enemy.

4) The mercy of God restores our relationship with Him.

5) The mercy of God attracts the goodness of God.

When God shows you His mercies, goodness begins to follow you. Psalm 23:6 says, ***"Surely goodness and mercy shall follow me all the days of my life, and I will dwell in the house of the LORD forever."***

The mercies of God have the power to completely rewrite a person's destiny. Even if others have written you off and believe nothing good can come from your life due to past mistakes and sins, the mercies of God bring about a change.

Just like Paul experienced a new beginning, and Rahab's past was transformed, the mercy of God has the capacity to change your life.

6) The mercy of God can reverse a

negative verdict.

In John 8:10-11, when Jesus encountered the woman caught in adultery, He said to her, *"Woman, where are those accusers of yours? Has no one condemned you?"* She replied, *"No one, Lord."* And Jesus said to her, *"Neither do I condemn you; go and sin no more."* Despite deserving death according to the law, mercy invaded her life, and the negative verdict was immediately reversed.

7) The mercy of God terminates judgment.

Micah 7:18 declares, *"Who is a God like unto thee, that pardoneth iniquity and passeth by the transgression of the remnant of his heritage? He retaineth not his anger forever, because he delighteth in mercy."*

8) The mercy of God opens the door of forgiveness.

God's mercy is greater than your sins. It is greater than all your iniquities and can forgive you of all your wrongdoings.

9) The mercy of God launches you into unquestionable blessings.

Psalm 67:1-2 says, *"God be merciful unto us and bless us, and cause His face to shine upon us, Selah. That Your way may be known on earth, Your salvation among all nations."*

You need to embrace the mercy of God and experience the restoration of your relationship with Him, the attraction of His goodness, the rewriting of your destiny, the reversal of negative verdicts, the termination of judgment, the opening of forgiveness, and the launch into unquestionable blessings.

10) The mercy of God is a platform for signs and wonders.

Matthew 20:30-34, in this passage, two blind men sitting by the roadside heard that Jesus was passing by and cried out, *"Have mercy on us, O Lord, thou Son of David."* The multitude rebuked them, but they cried out even more, seeking God's mercy. Jesus stopped, called them, and asked what they wanted Him to do for them. They replied, *"Lord, that our eyes may be opened."*

Jesus, filled with compassion, touched their eyes, and immediately they received their sight and followed Him. The power of God's mercies was manifested through the restoration of their eyesight. Through God's mercies, miracles become possible. The mercies of God serve as a doorway to signs and wonders. Wherever miracles occur, they are manifestations of God's mercies (Matthew 17:14-18).

11) The mercies of God act as a defense mechanism against satanic attacks

Genesis 31:22-29 expressly explains this. In this account, Laban pursued Jacob after learning of his departure. However, God appeared to Laban in a dream, warning him not to harm Jacob. Laban confronted Jacob, questioning his actions and accusing him of stealing away with Laban's daughters.

However, Laban acknowledged that God had instructed him not to speak either good or bad to Jacob. It is evident that God's mercies protected Jacob from harm and thwarted Laban's plans to cause him trouble.

Additionally, Psalm 57:3 says, ***"He shall send from heaven, and save me from the reproach of him that would swallow me up. Selah. God shall send forth his mercy and his truth."*** When God sends forth His mercies, Satan and his cohorts are left disappointed and unable to prevail against those who seek refuge in God's mercy.

The mercy of God serves as a powerful force that brings forth signs, wonders, and miraculous interventions. It acts as a shield against satanic attacks and brings deliverance to those who seek God's mercy. When God's mercies are released, His truth prevails, and His children are protected and saved from harm.

12) The mercy of God is the catalyst for answers to our prayers.

As expressed in Psalms 4:1 and Psalms 27:7. In Psalms 4:1, it is written, *"Hear me when I call, O God of my righteousness: you have relieved me in my distress; have mercy on me and hear my prayer."* Similarly, Psalms 27:7 states, *"Hear, O LORD, when I cry with my voice: have mercy on me and answer me."*

13) The mercy of God also provokes divine favour.

Receiving God's mercies inevitably leads to the enjoyment of His favor. The atmosphere of God's mercies has the power to generate favor in one's life. This truth is exemplified in Genesis 39:20-23, where

Joseph found himself confined in a prison as a result of his master's actions.

However, the LORD was with Joseph and extended His mercy towards him, ultimately bestowing favor upon him in the eyes of the prison keeper. Subsequently, the prison keeper entrusted Joseph with the responsibility of overseeing all the prisoners and their activities. Joseph's endeavors were blessed by the LORD, resulting in prosperity and success.

In conclusion, it is through the mercy of God that our prayers are answered, as evidenced by the verses in Psalms. Furthermore, this divine mercy has the power to attract favor from God, as illustrated by Joseph's story in Genesis 39:20-23.

Genesis 39:23 says, *"The keeper of the prison looked not to any thing that was under his hand; because the LORD was with him, and that which he did, the LORD made it to prosper."*

CHAPTER FIVE
HOW TO ACTIVATE THE MERCY OF GOD IN YOUR LIFE

"God never gets tired of forgiving us, but we are the ones who get tired of seeking His mercy." - George Patton

God's mercy is available to all, despite the fact that many have abused them to continue in sin. However, this does not prevent God's mercy from flowing to those who earnestly seek it. The purpose of God's mercy is to cleanse us from sin, not to enable us continue in sinful behaviours. Proverbs 16:6 says, *"By mercy and truth iniquity is purged: and by the fear of the LORD men depart from evil."* God does not desire His people to remain in partnership with the devil; rather, He seeks to sever that connection through His mercies.

STEPS TO EVOKE GOD'S MERCY

1) Acknowledge your sins:

The initial step to accessing God's mercy is to recognize and admit your sins. It is futile to fall into sin and pretend as if nothing has happened. We cannot deceive God, for everything we do in secret is laid bare before Him. God knows us better than we know ourselves.

Approach Him with honesty, humility, and sincerity of heart. You cannot be freed from your wrongdoings if you are not willing to acknowledge them. Similar to the prodigal son, forgiveness becomes attainable only when we realize the gravity of our actions.

Luke 15:17-18 says, ***"But when he came to himself, he said, 'How many hired servants of my father's have bread enough and to spare, and I perish with hunger! I will arise and go to my father, and will say unto him, "Father, I have sinned against heaven, and before thee."***

2) Confess and forsake your sins:

Proverbs 28:13 teaches us, ***"He that covereth his sins shall not prosper: but whoso confesseth and forsaketh them shall***

have mercy." In Luke 15:20-22, we see the prodigal son confessing his sins before his father, and as a result, he receives forgiveness.

When he was still a great distance away, his father saw him, was filled with compassion, and ran to embrace him, kissing him. The son said to him, *"Father, I have sinned against heaven and in thy sight, and am no more worthy to be called thy son."*

Yet, the father ordered his servants to bring forth the finest robe and put it on the son, and to put a ring on his hand and shoes on his feet. God is eager to forgive us if we are genuinely repentant. We must not take His mercies for granted. God's mercies can triumph over any sin and grant us a fresh start in our relationship with Him.

3) Seek God's mercy in any area you desire it;

The mercy of God is not exclusively for sinners; it is available to anyone who longs to experience the goodness of God. Psalm 23:6 declares, ***"Surely goodness and mercy shall follow me all the days of my life: and I will dwell in the house of the LORD forever."*** You can tap into the mercies of God in every aspect of your life.

When God shows you mercy, His goodness will pursue you. Just as David asked for mercy and received it, in Psalm 51:1 he pleads, ***"Have mercy upon me, O God, according to thy lovingkindness: according unto the multitude of thy tender mercies blot out my transgressions."***

4) Sow the seed of mercy:

Matthew 5:7 pronounces, ***"Blessed are the merciful: for they shall obtain mercy."*** If you show mercy to others, God will also show you mercy. Life operates according to the principles of sowing and reaping. If you sow mercy, you will reap God's mercies.

Galatians 6:7 warns, ***"Be not deceived; God is not mocked: for whatsoever a man soweth, that shall he also reap."*** Furthermore, in Matthew 18:23-35, Jesus tells the parable of a servant who was forgiven a massive debt by his master but refused to show mercy to a fellow servant who owed him a small amount.

As a consequence, the servant was handed over to tormentors. This parable emphasizes the importance of forgiving others from the heart in order to receive God's mercy. It is crucial to maintain a spirit of forgiveness towards others, as failing to do so may hinder the flow of God's mercy in our lives.

5) Cultivate a lifestyle of worship:

In Matthew 15:21-28, we encounter a Canaanite woman who approached Jesus, seeking mercy for her demon-possessed daughter. Initially, Jesus did not respond to her, but when she persisted in worship, acknowledging Him as Lord and seeking His help, Jesus commended her great faith and granted her request.

Genuine worship has the power to provoke God's mercies. Matthew 18:26-27 also illustrates how the act of worship from a servant moved the master with compassion, resulting in forgiveness. God never rejects true worship, and worshippers are positioned to receive His mercies. When worship is present, mercy flows abundantly towards worshippers.

6) Serve God wholeheartedly:

In Psalms 102:13-14, it is proclaimed that when individuals take pleasure in serving God, He arises to have mercy upon them. Those who are engaged in His business and are dedicated servants do not run out of God's mercies. A prime example is King David, whom God found as His servant, anointing him with holy oil.

God promised that His faithfulness and mercy would always be with David as long as he remained committed to serving Him.

Hence, God actively seeks those who serve Him to display His mercy. As we serve God faithfully, His mercies continue to accompany us.

7) Maintain a consistent prayer life:

Hebrews 4:16 encourages believers to approach the throne of grace with confidence, for in doing so, we find mercy and grace in our time of need. Prayer is the channel through which we access God's mercies.

The altar of prayer is the altar of mercies. By regularly spending time in prayer, you will not lack the mercies of God. Consistency in approaching the prayer altar ensures a continuous flow of God's mercies into your life.

HINDRANCES TO RECEIVING GOD'S MERCY

1) Self-condemnation

Revelation 12:10 reminds us that Satan, the accuser of the brethren. He tries to deceive us with lies and make us feel unworthy of God's mercy. He may bring up our past sins and attempt to convince us that forgiveness is unattainable.

However, we must reject these lies and focus on the mercies of God. Once we have repented of our sins, they no longer define us. It is essential to disregard the negative opinions of others and allow God's mercy to transform us.

Self-condemnation blocks the flow of God's mercies. Remember Romans 8:1,

"There is therefore now no condemnation to them which are in Christ Jesus, who walk not after the flesh, but after the Spirit."

2) Unforgiveness

Holding onto records of others' wrongs impedes our own ability to receive forgiveness from God. Jesus teaches us in Matthew 5:7 that the merciful will obtain mercy. We must practice forgiveness if we desire to be forgiven. Let go of bitterness and extend mercy to others, just as God has shown mercy to us.

3) Persistent disobedience

Persistent disobedience hinders the flow of God's mercies. It is inconsistent to expect God's mercies while intentionally continuing in sinful behaviour. We cannot have both sin and God's abundant mercy in our lives. True repentance involves turning away from disobedience and aligning ourselves with God's commands.

4) Unrepentant heart

Exodus 7:14 teaches us that hardening our hearts against sin disqualifies us from receiving God's mercies. We must be willing to acknowledge and repent of our sins to become recipients of His mercy. God's mercy is extended to those who demonstrate a genuine willingness to change.

Additional Scriptures on Mercy

- ✓ Numbers 14:18

- ✓ Deuteronomy 5:10, 7:9

- ✓ Nehemiah 9:31

- ✓ 2 Samuel 22:21

- ✓ 2 Chronicles 5:13

- ✓ Psalms 86:13, 31:16, 40:11, 52:8, 100:5, 123:8

- ✓ Isaiah 49:13, 55:7

- ✓ Jeremiah 30:18, 31:20

- ✓ Daniel 4:27

- ✓ Habakkuk 3:2

- ✓ 1 Peter 2:10

- ✓ Colossians 3:12

FINAL WORDS
EMBRACING GOD'S MERCY AND GRACE

"God's first response to our mistakes is mercy." - Pinterest

The mercy of God is inexhaustible; however, it should not be taken for granted. Mercy is an inherent aspect of God's character, consistently displayed from Genesis to Revelation. Without God's mercies, it is uncertain who would still be alive today. Romans 3:23 states, ***"For all have sinned and come short of the glory of God."***

David acknowledges that if God were to count our sins, no one would be able to stand (Psalms 130:3). The mercies of God have prevented the full effects of judgment from manifesting. It is unwise to wait until judgment arrives before seeking God's mercies. These mercies are available to you now, serving as a shield against the judgment you deserve.

Grasp onto His mercies, and that judgment will be eradicated. God is ready to forgive any sin, regardless of its magnitude. The weight of your sins, no matter how burdensome, can be rewritten by the mercies of God. Just as the mercies of God granted

David a fresh start, you too can experience a new beginning.

It is never too late to make things right. Regardless of how far you have strayed, a U-turn is still possible. You can overcome it. God's arms are wide open, ready to welcome you and transform your life through His mercies. Your past is not too tainted to be transformed by the mercies of God. As you reach out for it, God's mercies will grant you a new identity.

ABOUT THE BOOK

Unlock the breathtaking essence of divine mercy and discover a world where God's compassion knows no bounds. In the book, *"Becoming Vessels of His Mercy,"* you will witness the transformative power that awaits you, regardless of who you are, where you come from, or what your background or religion may be.

Drawing inspiration from Daniel 9:8, this captivating book unveils the profound truth that no one is beyond the reach of God's mercies. Regardless of your past mistakes or failures, the precious virtue of mercy is readily available to you.

Within these pages, you will uncover the true meaning of mercy, delving deep into the immense depths of God's merciful nature. Prepare to be enchanted by the myriad benefits that come with embracing divine mercy in your life.

But this book offers more than just knowledge. It provides practical guidance on how to obtain mercy in your everyday existence. You will be empowered with powerful strategies and transformative principles that will enable you to experience the life-changing effects of God's mercy firsthand.

Don't miss this remarkable opportunity to embrace the divine invitation that awaits you. Step into a realm where forgiveness, redemption, and grace abound. *"Becoming Vessels of His Mercy"* will leave you inspired, uplifted, and forever changed as you unlock the profound beauty and boundless love of God's mercy.